CONTENTS

ABOUT THE AUTHOR

John Cadogan's interest in study and the learning process developed from his own school and university experience and from coaching students through exams. While running his own secondary school tutoring business, he found himself continually repeating the same advice to his distraught students. In response to the misconceptions and general hysteria surrounding the subject of exams, he decided to formulate his ideas into a commonsense, good humoured guide to effective study.

John Cadogan lives and works in Australia.

GETTING INTO

EXAM SURVIVAL

John Cadogan

T R O T M A N

This edition published in 1994
by Trotman and Company Ltd,
12 Hill Rise, Richmond, Surrey TW10 6UA

© John Cadogan 1994

British Library Cataloguing in Publication Data
A catalogue record for this book is available from the British
Library.

ISBN 0 85660 247 7

Typeset by Type Study, Scarborough
Printed and bound in Great Britain

INTRODUCTION

☐ AUTHOR'S NOTE

Some people hate exams. They hate preparing for them. They hate actually doing them. And they hate waiting (sometimes for weeks, or months) to find out whether they've passed or failed.

In my own case I couldn't stand exams, but I had to get used to them. After completing my final year at secondary school and then seven years at university, I found, to my dismay, that I had endured between 85 and 100 exams. And before you say it . . . no, I was not a 'model' student. I passed, however, and was awarded the qualifications I sought. In the long run, that's all that counts.

Ask around: do you know anyone who actually likes exams? Neither do I. Such strange people may exist, but this book is written for the vast majority who hate exams but are forced to contend with them regardless.

There is no secret formula. The 'secret' to surviving exams, if there is one, is equal parts hard work and making the most of your available resources – including your time. It is not necessary to spend every waking hour studying. But some short-term lifestyle sacrifices are necessary, for the alternative is failure. I know from my own experiences, and those of my students, that you can succeed and still have some time to enjoy yourself.

The best thing about exams is when they're over – and you're sure you've passed. This book won't reveal how to enjoy exams – I don't believe that's possible. However, it will reveal how to get the marks you need – a far more important subject.

☐ WHY BOTHER?

Life would be a lot more fun without exams. They are an unfortunate reality. But they're the biggest hurdle between where you are and where you want to be.

Teachers and parents are always trying to compel you to improve your marks. In fairness, they only do that because they care about you.

But this alone is not a good enough reason to want to get better marks. You're not studying for other people, you're doing it for you! You are the one who'll benefit if you pass. You'll be at a terrible disadvantage if you fail. The consequences of your performance affects you directly, and others only indirectly. So, even if you resent everyone's constant urging to do better, don't deliberately under-perform to spite them. You'll only be hurting yourself . . .

The very fact that you are studying something means that you have a goal. Say to yourself: 'Why am I doing this?' Do you want to finish school with a wide range of options, get into a particular course at a particular university or college, do well in your final degree, or are you after a good job or promotion in your present job? These goals account for the overwhelming majority of students' reasons for studying.

So why are you doing it? Whatever the reason, don't worry what other people think of it – the only person who has to care about it is you. In fact, write it down: 'I want to . . . (study law at university, or whatever)'. Scrawl it on cardboard, in big letters, and stick it up on the wall at eye level, just in front of your study desk. It will be your personal reminder to try hard.

Before going any further, we should examine the 'easy' alternative: Wouldn't it be better just to slack off, have fun and forget about exams? Maybe . . . but these benefits exist only in the short term; you could avoid the pressure and have fun for a few weeks, or even months, and then regret it for the rest of your life.

INTRODUCTION

Think about it – academic qualifications usually go hand-in-hand with many lifestyle benefits, including interesting work, community respect and, importantly, more pay.

This book is aimed at anyone taking exams in any subject; whether several subjects will be taken together such as for those sitting for GCSEs or A-levels, or for those just taking a single exam. The pressure of exams can affect anyone, whether they are at school or are a part-time mature student taking an evening class or a further vocational qualification. The advice given will help you to be better organised and more confident with both your study preparation and how you tackle the exam on the day.

For those of you who are keen to try and succeed, the time to work hard is now! Make your choice, and do it right now, before it's too late. You can hate exams, or get angry or upset with them – whatever seems appropriate. But the one thing you must do is pass them.

UNDERSTANDING EXAMS

How much do you know about exams? If you're a normal student, the answer to this question will probably be: 'Not much'. Unfortunately, most of us are stuck with formal examinations until someone devises a better, universally accepted system.

Exams are a tool for gauging how well you understand the things you've been taught. They take place because teachers and lecturers can't reasonably expect a truly objective answer if they merely ask you how well you understand the topics covered by the syllabus; they need more proof.

You don't have to like exams. What you must do is work hard enough to get the marks you need. If you work consistently, you will succeed. (Don't panic, however – you can still find time for your other commitments or do whatever it is that you enjoy – your outside life is quite safe.)

Exams aren't a perfect means of assessing how much you've learned. It's still possible to receive quite poor marks even if you have an above-average understanding of the work. This could easily happen if you misinterpret the questions, or run out of time, or make mistakes because you're under pressure and working much faster than normal.

Everyone has, at one time or another, looked over their marked solutions to a particular exam, only to find many so-called 'stupid' errors. In other words, forced errors which, under 'normal' circumstances, you wouldn't make. It's terribly frustrating because you clearly understood the question, knew the required theory and how to frame a correct answer – but for some reason, a mistake happened and you lost valuable marks.

Forced errors are one of the most common ways for otherwise good students to lose marks. But exams don't differentiate between people who make forced errors and people who just don't understand the work. One factor alone is the cause: inadequate preparation. If you don't work hard, you will look stupid. If you work hard, but in the wrong way, you may well also look stupid. Some people may enjoy the studying part of the preparation, but be totally unprepared as far as exam skills are concerned. Others, who may have limited study and revision time, may manage this time inadequately and find they have left it too late. If you don't get the required marks, you can forget about achieving your goal – and that's a very depressing situation. In order to maximise your marks, you need to understand the work and develop other skills that allow you to demonstrate your knowledge during the exam.

The solution is simple: be motivated, keep reading. Learn how to prepare effectively and then practise as often as possible. This book is full of suggestions for effective preparation. These can be adapted to exams in all subjects. Consider each, and apply those which you think will help.

Some students want high marks. Some want merely to pass with minimal effort. Which kind of student are you? Decide now, but first consider the result you need. Sometimes it is essential to excel; at other times, passing is sufficient.

Example

There are only 600 places available on a particular course at university but there are 12,000 students taking the entrance exam. If you are one of these candidates, you will only be successful if your marks fall in the top five per cent. This would be a good example of a situation in which it is important to try your hardest.

Five years later, you are sitting for your final examination at university. If you pass, you will have earned your degree. If you get 99 per cent, your degree will be the same as if you had passed with 60 per cent. You only need to pass, but how hard you actually try is up to you.

So, should you bother? How hard should you try? Is it all worth it later on? Every student will ask themselves that. Then, when it's all over, for those that pass the answer is 'yes'. The minority who fail answer 'no' – clearly for them it is a waste of time. But if you want to be able to say 'yes, it was horrible but worthwhile', it's time to put your decision into action and start working now.

SUMMARY

1. **Exams are a necessary evil.**
2. **Getting the marks you need doesn't mean giving up fun altogether – but some sacrifices are necessary.**
3. **Hard work and effective preparation are the key factors.**
4. **If you want to succeed, make the commitment and start working now!**

☐ THE SKILLS

Knowing the subject matter is vital. You cannot disguise inadequate preparation with a repertoire of trick exam skills. Why do you think most of your face-to-face teaching time is devoted to learning aspects of the work? No matter how clever you are, if you don't understand the work, your poor marks will make you look stupid.

These are the skills you'll need in order to realise your full potential:

Subject knowledge

You must know, well in advance, precisely what topics will be covered in the exam. Not only that, a good 'working knowledge' of these topics is essential. Some students are content to know the theory only, but a working knowledge of the subject means knowing how to answer the questions by applying the relevant theory. In the science subjects, this involves a familiarity with solving problems. In the humanities area, you must be able to formulate essay-style answers in the required format, supported by the theory. It's very different from merely knowing dates, quotes and equations, although you will still need to remember these!

Comprehension

If you don't understand the questions, how can you get any marks at all? Comprehension is essential. You need to pick from the question exactly what the examiner wants you to do. Then you have to sift through all the other information and get from the question to the first line of your answer. Comprehension is the skill of identifying what is required in your answer and what information you are given to work with.

Speed

If you only answer half of the questions, what is the best mark you can hope for? Fifty per cent – and only then if you don't make a single mistake. In an exam, you can only earn marks for the answers you supply, so you must work at a pace which allows you to complete all of the questions within the time limit. And that usually means working much faster than normal. However, working at exam pace must not interfere with your accuracy.

Accuracy

If you understand the question and apply your sound working knowledge of the theory, you should get full marks. However, the need for accuracy is vital when you're under pressure. With the right kind of practice, the number of forced errors you commit can be reduced. Nevertheless you would be surprised at the number of times examiners have seen students write things like: $3 + 4 = 12$.

Neatness

Many people clearly believe that presentation does not significantly affect their final marks. They are wrong. If there are two papers with the same answers on them, the neat one always gets more marks. Why?

In a science exam, if your answer is neat and you make a mistake half-way through, it's easy for you to check your working and correct it. If you can't find the mistake, the examiner will find it and award you some marks for the correct part of your answer. But if your answer is wrong and the examiner can't understand the working, you won't get any marks. And it's much harder for you to check your own working if it's untidy.

If two essays were almost identical, the neat one gets more marks because it seems far less disjointed – the examiner doesn't have to keep stopping to work out what's been written.

Neatness means more than just having clear handwriting. It involves using clear margins on both sides of the page (and at the top and bottom), arranging thoughts into sentences and paragraphs, using correct punctuation and, for scientific answers, setting out a logical progression for the solution as you work down the page.

SUMMARY

1. **Knowing the subject matter is vital.**
2. **There is more to being good at exams than just knowing the subject matter.**
3. **The key areas to address are: knowledge, comprehension, speed, accuracy, and neatness.**

EXAM PREPARATION

There are two ways of dealing with the problem of exam preparation. One way is to not think about it very much – do your assigned homework and hope for the best. The alternative is to make the most of your resources. In other words, consider what exams are actually like, and modify your study programme so that you train yourself to maximise your comprehension, speed, accuracy and neatness as well as your knowledge. This second option will allow you to cope easily with major exams.

Preparing for an important exam is like training for the final of a sporting competition. The only difference is that you will be competing in an intellectual rather than a physical arena. Champion swimmers practise by swimming long distances. The top cricket teams spend many hours each week playing cricket. Of course, these champions do supplementary training, too. Most would do some weight training at a gym. But the most important aspect of their training is repetition of the actual event in which they compete. There is an important lesson here for people about to sit exams.

There is a 'secret' to being good at anything – repetition. You don't have to be a 'natural'. It certainly helps if you are naturally gifted – but try naming one sporting champion who doesn't train hard. There simply aren't any. This doesn't only apply to sport, because all skills can be improved with practice.

If you have ever seen someone working at a trade, like a skilled bricklayer doing their job, it can look easy – until you try it yourself. That's when you find there's more to turning a pile of bricks and mortar into a wall than meets the eye. You could read a book on laying bricks, then devote all your attention to the job and listen to the right advice while you're doing it, but you'll still do a comparatively bad job. On the other hand, an experienced person could listen to the radio, talk to colleagues and still do a professional job. There is no substitute for experience.

With exams, you must really want to improve. If reaching your goal is important to you – and it should be – that should be all the motivation you need. But the hands-on part of getting better at exams involves nothing more than repetition – the more you practise, the more you improve.

Another important parallel between athletes and students is that all serious athletes review and correct any mistakes they may have made during training or at previous competitions. This applies particularly to students. What do you think would happen to your marks if you did exams all the time and then conducted a regular review aimed at correcting your mistakes?

Clearly you can't do exams all the time so the next best thing is to study under exam conditions whenever possible (see p. 15). But don't worry, studying like this doesn't take any longer than 'conventional' study (whatever that is), so the threat to your social life is minimal. Your available time is simply made far more productive than before. And that means you can expect to see your marks improve dramatically.

If you think that preparing for exams involves opening the textbook and merely reading it or doing a lot of problems or essays, perhaps with as much of your brain switched off as possible, get set for a shock. For a start, it's quite different from actually doing an exam. And while it may work for a handful of extremely gifted students, those of us who have to work a bit harder to get what we want will have to start helping ourselves by making our revision a bit more sensible.

At some stage, everyone experiences a 'bad' exam. Maybe, for example, the questions are totally different from those in the textbook or there is much more work than you could possibly complete in the available time. If it hasn't happened to you yet . . . it probably will! But don't hit the panic button – there are quite a few strategies you can use to combat 'bad' exams.

SUMMARY

1. **Make the most of your resources.**
2. **Preparing for exams is just like training for a sport.**
3. **The 'secret' is repetition.**
4. **Review and correct your past mistakes.**
5. **Effective study means using more than just the textbook.**

☐ LEARNING

One prerequisite of exam success is that you must remember a great deal of the appropriate information. You should first understand the processes by which you learn and recall the various bits of information. Then, you will be able to remember more easily the right information at the right time.

Here again, it doesn't matter what the subject is; the more of it you do, the better at it you'll get and the more of it you'll remember at a later date. If a particular topic proves to be a major upset, beat it by tackling it more aggressively than the others. While studying, answer as many questions on it as you possibly can. You won't enjoy it very much (especially at the beginning) but your ability will improve.

Consider two things: Your phone number and what you had for dinner on Tuesday night three weeks ago. Unless that particular Tuesday was significant because it was your birthday, or some other special day, you'll know your phone number, but not what you ate that night. All of us make a subconscious decision to remember some things, but not others. You have decided that your phone number is important enough to store in your long-term memory. That meal three weeks ago went into your short-term memory. And after a few hours, or at most a few days, it just disappeared.

11

Everyone's senses are assailed with millions of bits of information all day, every day. And there has to be some mechanism for separating the things that are important enough to remember from the things that aren't. Otherwise, you would quickly have a head full of useless junk. How useful would it be if you clearly remembered that the milk in the refrigerator was bad on 11 December 1982, and the date and time of your first dentist's appointment in 1978, but you ran out of the room to remember your own name? Your consciousness is not actively involved with this process, it happens automatically.

The best place for the information you need to survive exams is in your long-term memory. When you look at the questions in an exam, wouldn't it be nice if the required theory just popped up inside your head, immediately, with no effort or guesswork required? You can achieve this by being very familiar with the work over a long period. That is, by repetition commencing months before the exam. You can supplement this by some intensive revision around exam time (which helps reinforce short-term memory), but be aware that short-term memory alone is not enough. That's why 'cramming' before exams never works. Your revision must take place frequently, over a long period.

Use more than one sense when you study – sound as well as sight; and different media – such as pictures and diagrams as well as text. Some subjects, such as languages or classics of literature or some history themes, may mean that you have access to recorded information or perhaps films on video. If you can use these resources constructively it may help to vary your study pattern in a creative way. If you are merely reading, it's terribly easy for your mind to wander all over the place. Have you ever glanced up after reading a complete block of text, only to discover that you were thinking about something completely different? *When this happens, YOU ARE NOT STUDYING.*

Recruit as many senses as possible to play an active part in your studying. It's easy: read and take notes at the same time. Read relevant bits of theory out loud, as you're writing them down (this works best when you're alone – for obvious reasons). Write down the required theory not once, but many times. Each time you answer a mathematics-style question, write down the relevant theory (do this in the exam also). It's very easy to daydream when you're only reading – using just one sense – but it's impossible when you're doing two (or three) things at once. But if you're so intelligent that you can simultaneously read, write, speak and daydream, nothing in this book will be of any use to you.

SUMMARY

1. **Repetition is the key to learning anything.**
2. **Use your long-term memory.**
3. **Recruit more than one sense while you study.**
4. **Cramming for exams never works!**

☐ STUDY THE RIGHT WAY!

Preparing for an important exam by reading the textbook, or just answering questions from it, is like a footballer preparing for the cup final by only jogging around a track. Clearly, it's not a very authentic simulation of the actual competition.

If you insist exclusively on reading or answering questions from the textbook, you'll have to contend with these problems:

1. The textbook's topics are arranged in a logical order. In an exam, they are not. The logical order is an advantage for learning, but it doesn't help students of mathematics and related subjects because it's immediately obvious to you which topic you are revising. In the exam, your first job is to decide which topic the question relates to and then which specific pieces of theory must be used to answer the questions. The logical order of the textbook removes any opportunity for you to develop this skill.

2. The theory in the textbook is usually printed very close to the relevant questions. You can easily refer to quotes, equations and examples. This, also, is excellent for learning the work, but it's not much help when you're preparing for an exam. There are usually no helpful quotes, equations or examples printed in exams. You are required to use your memory. If you are lazy – and all of us are, to some degree – you should realise that if you rely on the textbook's theory and not your memory, you may not be able to remember vital pieces of theory in the exam.

3. Questions in textbooks may be worded differently from those in exams. In mathematics and other sciences, there is no single, universal terminology. This can lead to major problems interpreting exam questions. And if you can't interpret a question, you won't even be able to start on it. And the examiner won't be able to award you any marks.

4. You probably dislike certain topics within one subject. Or, worse, you may not be particularly impressed with a whole subject. Textbooks make it very easy to avoid these topics or subjects by working around them. The topics you hate are worth marks, just like the topics you like. Don't ever say: 'I'll study that topic tomorrow'. Inevitably you won't get around to it!

5. Everyone likes to work at a comfortable pace. But when was the last time you felt that the pace was comfortable in an exam? If you want to complete all the questions, you will be forced to work faster than 'comfortable' during exams. You can improve your exam pace without sacrificing accuracy, but you have to practise. How will you know when you're fast enough? Not by using the textbook, that's for sure! Exam preparation is the same as training for a marathon – if you don't train, you won't finish!

SUMMARY

Never rely on the textbook!

☐ THE EXAM ENVIRONMENT

The exam environment is very different from the day-to-day school or college environment, and equally different from the 'normal' study environment. Firstly, the stress involved when doing an exam is particularly high. You will be required to work very fast if you are to complete all the questions. If you make errors because you are under pressure, you will lose marks just the same as if you didn't know the work.

The exam environment is worse than unpleasant: it's horrible. You must, however, try to simulate exam conditions while you study. If you do it often enough, exams begin to seem less like torture and more like hard work.

These suggestions will help you duplicate exam conditions while you study:

1. Make your study room relatively quiet. Exams are always done under quiet, but not silent, conditions. This is easy to achieve if you have a separate room set aside for study, though this may not always be possible. Don't make it too quiet because there's always some annoying little noise in the exam room. If you're really unlucky, builders may be operating heavy machinery right next door.

2. Try to arrange a dedicated study location. In other words, an area set aside for study alone. A simple desk and cupboard space in a bedroom will suffice. Don't store other things in your study area. CDs, magazines and other distracting items are far more attractive than study and are therefore not allowed!

3. Don't play music or watch television while you study. You can't do either in an exam. More importantly, any attempt to make study more enjoyable will reduce its effectiveness. If you reduce the distractions to an absolute minimum, you may find yourself concentrating on the work. After all, there won't be anything more enjoyable to think about.

4. Make sure that the room you study in is well-ventilated, well-lit and not too warm or cool. Bad lighting makes concentration very difficult. Warm, stuffy rooms are great for falling asleep in, but no good for study. Try to keep your study desk uncluttered and well organised. You may well think this suggestion is a waste of space, but the wrong conditions make it impossible to concentrate; for most of us, it's hard enough to concentrate when the conditions are perfect.

5. There are no rest periods during exams. Many final exams are three hours in length. If you normally revise your work in blocks of 30 minutes, a three-hour exam will be a 600 per cent shock to your system! It is therefore vital to ensure your concentration span is up to the task at hand. For three weeks, try increasing the duration of your study blocks by 15 minutes. Then add another 15 minutes for another three weeks. Initially, it may be difficult to concentrate for the extra time. Don't give up, your concentration span will gradually increase. Motivation has a lot to do with it – you probably don't have much trouble concentrating on the latest video release, or even two in a row. You should sit for the occasional three-hour exam simulations in your study time (say at least one a week) so that you will be prepared for the duration of the upcoming exams.

6. You will usually be denied access to theory during exams. (Don't even consider cheating! Even if you're unconcerned with the moral implications of cheating, you will be caught – and the penalties are extreme.) Some science papers include a data sheet, and while this provides some elementary theory or physical constants which are hard to remember, it isn't much help. Do not assume that the data sheet will be a big help – it's not like a textbook, so you won't be able to study and do the exam at the same time. If you don't understand the work, the data will be useless. Before you sit for an exam, make sure you can complete the questions without access to the theory. Do it by including regular revision sessions without referring to the theory. This is also the best way of indicating topics you don't properly understand.

SUMMARY

1. **Try to simulate the exam environment whenever you study: quiet, uncluttered, no television or music, and good lighting and ventilation.**
2. **Work hard at improving your attention span.**
3. **Don't rely on the textbook for theory – use your memory instead.**

☐ USING PAST EXAM PAPERS

Should you do past exam papers? Is it worth the extra effort? Yes, definitely – do them as often as possible. You are particularly fortunate if you are in your final year of school, or at university, because there are usually many sources of past papers, and they often come complete with the required answers and working. ('Mock' exams for GCSEs, for example, are obviously a good way of getting practice at the real thing!)

Here's why you should take advantage of past papers:

1. You will become familiar with the terminology used in the exam. As discussed earlier, this may be quite different from that used in your textbooks or class notes.

2. You can easily simulate exam conditions by doing past papers within the exam's time limit and without access to theory. You will be able to assess your ability to work at the required pace and your understanding of the subject.

3. You can't omit topics by accident or on purpose (because you simply don't like them). Past papers address every theory area and you should attempt to answer all of the questions. This forces you to become conversant with topics that you would have otherwise planned to do 'tomorrow', but never quite got around to.

4. If you have access to the correct answers, you can mark the papers you've completed. Then you can do what the professional athletes do – review your performance and correct any errors by directing your study programme towards areas that need more work.

5. You will become familiar with the general structure of the paper, the number of questions and so on, and the layout of the exams in each subject you are studying. If you complete many past papers, you will know basically what to expect when you sit for the real thing. The vast majority of exams present very similar questions every year. There is a very good reason for this: in some cases there are few new developments in subjects in both the sciences and the humanities. Students of literature, for example, may find that a text they are studying has been set two or more years ago, particularly in the case of 'classics' and, of course, Shakespeare. Those taking mathematics will find, for example, that the theories and practical exercises of geometry and calculus (which after all have been in existence for hundreds of years) will involve few changes from one year's paper to the next.

6. Being familiar with the content of many past exams, and being confident of your ability to understand the questions and complete them within the time limit removes the fear of the unknown from your exam preparation. It's a huge boost to your confidence and it reduces the stress you experience before and during the exam. And because you'll feel a little more relaxed, you'll probably even make fewer mistakes.

SUMMARY

Past papers solve many study problems.

☐ PREPARING AND USING SUMMARIES

Some students become obsessed with summaries of the work

covered in class. Quite a common mistake is to spend far too much time preparing and re-writing summaries of the work. Some students even go to the extreme of never doing anything else. Summaries have their place – they're an essential reference guide when you're looking for a piece of theory, like a quote or an equation, in a hurry. Rewriting summaries is an effective way to 'over-learn' names, quotes, dates, places, events and equations, etc. Rewriting summaries exclusively is not an effective revision system, however. It's not particularly good training for answering exam questions. The only exam question you would be training yourself for is: 'Summarise the geography (or whatever) syllabus'.

SUMMARY

Don't rely exclusively on theory summaries.

☐ STUDY TIME

You have only limited time to devote to studying. Everyone needs to relax and have fun, plus find time for the routine, domestic jobs and commitments that don't disappear just because you're a student. More than being just acceptable, needing some time to unwind after lectures or work is essential. Effective study demands the right frame of mind, and if you haven't had any time to relax, yours will be wrong. You do, however, need to place this in perspective: four hours in front of the television is definitely excessive.

Write a list of exactly what you spend your time doing, every day for a week. Add up the time spent sleeping, working, actively pursuing your interests, and the time you spent doing nothing specific. You'll probably shock yourself when you see how much time you spend doing nothing worthwhile. This is where you can get your extra time for revision from. Do you travel on the train, or by bus, for an hour or more each day? Since you're already confined, this is a perfect opportunity for study. Do you baby-sit regularly? Do you have free time between lectures or classes? Have you been staring mindlessly at the television for two or three hours at a stretch? Studying during these periods won't cramp your style since you won't be missing out on anything more important while doing so.

If you get home at 4.00pm and go to bed at 11.00pm, you only control this block of seven hours each day. Chances are the rest of your day is already rigidly organised – get up, dress, eat, travel to class, lectures or work, take part in the day's activities, travel home . . . freedom! Or at least a bit of flexibility in the schedule. You must, however, relax, handle the domestic tasks, enjoy yourself and study in this time. Assuming relaxation, chores, and recreation take up an average of four hours, perhaps three hours remains for study. As major exams approach it's reasonable to expect an increase to say four hours or more per night (and more at the weekend). Of course you are allowed regular sport or a part-time job or whatever. Simply compensate for this time by increasing your study on the days when you're not otherwise committed. For those with a full-time job, it is of course more difficult, and more sacrifices will have to be made.

It is much more important to study productively than it is to spend hours sitting at your desk kidding yourself by merely going through the motions. Never go to your room with the intention of studying for an hour when, really, all you're going to do is this:

Organise desk, sharpen pencils	5 minutes
Decide what to study	5 minutes
Make cup of coffee	5 minutes
Arrange books and paper	5 minutes
Flick through books, do some problems	15 minutes
Look out window daydreaming	10 minutes
Do more problems, slowly	10 minutes
Pack up equipment, tidy up	5 minutes
TOTAL	1 hour

If this is you, you managed to spend less than half the time actually studying. Why not just work hard for 25 minutes and spend the rest of the time relaxing? That would certainly be just as effective, and more relaxing. Many students study this way – do you? If so, you are kidding yourself! Particularly if you actually believe you are studying productively. If you've already decided to put the whole hour aside, or any other worthwhile period of time, then be organised and spend the whole hour actually studying! Sitting at a desk, kidding yourself that you are studying for any length of time is anything but a guarantee of good marks.

Good marks are ensured only by effective study, and that's a rather individual thing. There is no single, universally effective study programme. People respond differently to various study methods. If you've found some techniques that are effective for you, keep doing them. Don't stop just because someone tells you that they won't work, when clearly they do work. Some students go to sleep as soon as they get home, wake up just as everyone else is going to bed and study for a few hours, when it's quiet, before going back to sleep. Others may think they're crazy (because most people wouldn't be able to study like this) but it appears to work for them.

Having said that, effective study programmes do have common elements, and there are a few things that never work. Studying in front of the TV never works. Neither does playing loud music while studying. Forget also, the so-called 'group' study, or study sitting on the beach, or in the park. They all sound pretty enjoyable, don't they? They're also universally hopeless when it comes to preparing effectively for exams. There are actually many other methods you can employ to make your study enjoyable. Unfortunately, they all make it less effective.

Studying is not an enjoyable experience for most people, though it is worse for some than for others. For most students, unless they are in the unusual situation of having a total and continuing fascination for their subject area, serious study is an unpleasant activity. Most students hate it. This is a normal reaction. You'll just have to press on in spite of the difficulties. You must develop the self-discipline to work hard at it regardless.

Face facts: the more enjoyable you make study, the less like real study it is. What really counts when you study is determined, individual effort. Why not organise your time better and study productively for a sensible length of time? Three hours of determined, concentrated effort is infinitely better than kidding yourself for six. Commit yourself and go for it, then play loud music, fade out in front of the television or visit your friends later. At least then you'll be able to enjoy yourself with a clear conscience. And if you have other commitments at least you will have used your limited time more productively.

Whatever sensibly productive time you decide to spend studying each day should be split into two areas of equal importance: homework and revision.

SUMMARY

1. **Allocate your study time sensibly.**
2. **Concentrated effort counts.**
3. **Enjoyable modifications to study usually don't work.**
4. **Both homework and revision are vital.**

☐ HOMEWORK

Homework is not a cheap attempt by educators to make your home life terribly unpleasant, it's set to reinforce the work done in class. Without it, you would quickly lose the plot. Don't let the homework assignments 'snowball' on you. A great many students have a relaxed few weeks and then panic when they realise there are four assignments due within a few days. Get into the habit of completing homework assignments as soon as possible after they are set. Never leave them until the night before they're due.

Homework is vital, not optional, as some students apparently believe. There is usually some minor penalty imposed if you fail to complete it. Some homework, in the shape of essays and assignments, often counts towards your final assessment. But keep in mind also that the real penalty for not doing your homework is not understanding the work, and the poor exam marks that result. You can, and should, use your set homework to improve the related skills such as accuracy, neatness and comprehension. You'll be doing your homework anyway, so it makes sense to develop your skills in these areas at the same time.

In addition to your homework, set some time aside each day for revision early on. How much time depends on many factors including the current homework load, the number of subjects you are studying and your ability. Your revision must address every topic in every subject on a regular basis. If you don't, you will quickly forget everything that could be of use during an exam. Either you'll fail, or you'll have to quickly re-learn some topics as the exams approach. In that case, you'll be cramming facts into your short-term memory, not relying on your (far more reliable) long-term memory. If you revise regularly, over a long period, all the useful aspects of the work will work their way into your long-term memory.

SUMMARY

1. Remember, some homework often counts towards your final assessment.
2. Use regular homework to develop the exam skills of comprehension, accuracy and neatness.
3. Regular homework helps your long-term memory.

☐ REVISION

If it is to be effective, revision must be done regularly. Draw up a comprehensive revision timetable and stick to it. Allocate some time every day for revision – starting today! The big question for those taking more than one exam is: How do you divide your

revision time equitably between the various subjects you're
studying? For a start, write each subject on a sheet of paper.
Rate them in order of most enjoyable to least enjoyable. Decide
how much time you're prepared to allocate for revision and
divide it equally between each subject. Then modify your list
according to these factors:

1. Are all the subjects worth equal value as far as your final
assessment is concerned? If some are worth more, increase the
time you'll spend on those, according to the subject's greater
worth. For example, in your assessment, mathematics may be
worth 150 marks while the other subjects may each be worth
100. You should then devote at least half as much time again to
mathematics compared to the others.

2. Some subjects intrinsically require more or less study. Some
you may find comparatively easy. These are probably on top of
your list – the most enjoyable subjects. You can probably still
perform well in these subjects' exams with a bit less revision
than the others. Some you may hate and do poorly at unless you
increase the amount of revision spent on them.

3. How close are the exams? If they're still a couple of months
off, don't worry. But you must increase your total revision time
as the exams draw closer. Eight weeks before major exams, try
doing an extra hour of revision per day. Then, with only four
weeks to go, add another hour. This is far more effective than
only bothering to add four hours per day in the week before the
exams.

Adjust the time allocated for each subject on your list
accordingly. But remember that, unless the exams are soon, the
total time you allocate should be the same as that which you
started with.

Give your revision programme a go for a few weeks and then
reassess the total time you think is necessary, and the way in
which you've divided it between the subjects. You'll quickly be
able to improve on the way you've set it up. You'll only improve if
you revise the work regularly. The earlier you start, the higher
your marks will be. Just remember, the aim isn't to make study
more enjoyable – you're trying to make it more effective. You're

doing it for one reason only – to achieve your goal. Stick to your revision programme. Don't kill yourself, just pour in the concentrated effort for the required time and then relax.

Homework and revision become much, much easier if you have a complete set of neat class notes for each subject. Keep your notes up to date! If you miss a class, for whatever reason, get copies of the notes from someone who was there. File your notes for each subject in separate folders. Use a folder that holds all the sheets of paper firmly in place. Make a neat summary of the relevant theory at logical intervals, for example at the beginning of each new chapter in the textbook. And improve your access to the individual topics with the intelligent use of chapter dividers. One more thing: don't wait three months before filing new notes away. Do it at the end of each week.

If your notes are untidy and it takes 15 minutes to find any one particular item of information, that time spent wasn't 'studying' at all, it was a frustrating waste of time. If your notes are really poor, help yourself by asking a teacher (or anyone else who may know) if you need help with your note-taking or note-keeping skills. If you seriously want help it usually isn't too hard to find.

Much of your revision should be spent doing as many past exam papers as possible. These should be done at exam pace, and marked after your revision session. Then look at what you got wrong. Answer questions from textbooks or other sources when your performance review indicates a weakness in a particular area. Don't ignore your weaknesses because you can't get any marks for topics that you don't understand. If you really don't understand a topic then ask someone about it! Most teachers are more than happy to help students who demonstrate nothing more than a serious desire to learn. They're usually thrilled when they discover that someone has actually taken an interest in studying 'their' subject. (Don't worry, your reputation will be safe – they won't tell your friends that you've been studying . . . !)

One last thing: make a list of topics covered in each subject. Each time you do a past exam question, put a tick next to the relevant topic(s) on your list. After some time, this will show you which topics have been receiving more or less attention.

SUMMARY

1. **Effective revision must be frequent and regular.**
2. **Make a revision timetable and stick to it.**
3. **Maintain a set of neat, accurate notes.**
4. **Be organised!**

☐ YOUR PAST PERFORMANCE

What do you do with your exam papers once they've been marked? Take special care to hide them from your parents? Throw them away – quickly? Conveniently lose them . . . in the open fireplace, or the shredder? The one thing you must do is use them as a guide to improving your performance in the next exam. Don't recriminate over a bad result – use it to do better next time around. It's easy to do and it doesn't take very long, so give it a go:

Step 1

Evaluate your marks in each question. Make a list of the ways you lost marks, tabulated in the following way:

- How many marks did you get in total?

- How many marks did you lose because you didn't understand the theory?

- How many marks did you lose because you made a forced error in your answer?

- How many marks did you lose because you couldn't interpret a question or because you answered a different question to the one which was asked?

- How many marks did you lose because you ran out of time?

Step 2

What factors caused you to lose significant marks? 'Significant

26

marks' means anything more than about eight per cent, indicating a flaw in the way you approach exams. Tackle these flaws in the following way:

1. If your list indicates that you don't understand some of the theory, increase your knowledge by revising the topic(s) and answering as many questions on these topics, from the textbook and elsewhere, as possible.

2. If you made a lot of forced errors, you need to improve your accuracy. Complete a lot of questions at exam pace. This will give you more practise at working faster than usual and it won't hurt your concentration span, either. These two factors combined make up your accuracy.

3. If you couldn't interpret some of the questions, you must practise a technique for interpreting difficult questions, particularly those that are initially very hard to understand. There's a section on this at the end of Chapter 3.

4. If you ran out of time, you must increase the speed at which you work. Here again, practising past papers at exam pace (i.e. within the time limit) is ideal. Don't have any rest periods in the middle of these papers. Keep practising and your speed will improve without adversely affecting your accuracy.

SUMMARY

1. Constructively analyse your past exams – learn by your mistakes.
2. Don't let your weaknesses beat you. Identify them and tackle them. They can be overcome.

☐ STRESS

Stress is real. Suffering from stress while preparing for exams is simply not funny. Some stress is unavoidable – it goes with the territory. A little stress may even be helpful. You should, however, realise that too much stress is counterproductive. Apart from making your life a misery, your exam performance will suffer if you don't do something about it.

Here's a few suggestions for reducing stress:

1. Try improving your diet. Seriously, a poor diet can leave you feeling washed out, completely devoid of energy. That makes it very hard to study; you won't feel motivated and your concentration span will be terrible. It's a well documented medical fact that the 'average' diet in most western countries is too high in fat and simple sugars. And, as a population, we don't eat enough complex carbohydrate.

If you feel washed out all the time, cut down on things like soft drink, cakes, sweets, ice cream and fast food. Substitute these with fresh fruit, bread, rice, vegetables, milk and fruit juice. It sounds boring, but isn't. (Regardless of what various advertisements infer, vitamin pills are not the answer. Healthy eating is. If you're not vitamin deficient, extra vitamins won't help. Most can't be stored, and they pass straight through your system.) You don't have to stop eating this kind of stuff altogether, just arrange things so that your junk-food intake changes from frequent to occasional. If you really enjoy eating junk-food treat yourself occasionally, not every day. Try healthy eating during the week and, if you must, binge at the weekend.

2. If you're finding it hard to sleep, even though you're really tired, that's a sure sign of suffering from too much stress. Listen to these messages your body sends you from time to time. If you're really tired, your body is telling you that it needs rest: obviously, the best thing to do is go to sleep. (But tackling real insomnia may be difficult; you may have to alter your daily regime or seek further help: relaxation techniques and/or exercise plans will be necessary.)

Why are you so tired? If you think it's because there's too much work to do, then it's fair to say that you've organised yourself badly. The usual response to this accusation is: 'But this assignment/exam/presentation is due tomorrow!'. If you work toward these assignments systematically, over a sensible period, then last minute blitzes aren't necessary. Nobody has to push themselves to the absolute limits of physical endurance or turn their lives into purgatory in order to succeed.

The secret is simple: get yourself organised. Pour in the concentrated, determined effort for a sensible part of each day. Work very hard during that time and then spend a few hours enjoying yourself – you'll deserve it!

3. Don't drink coffee or take other stimulants, particularly at night. Caffeine is the most commonly used stimulant in our society. Drinking coffee, tea or Coke, or eating chocolate is an excellent way of increasing the caffeine in your system. Don't make it harder than necessary for your body to relax. If you are finding it hard to sleep, try cutting out coffee, Coke and chocolate altogether. If you can't do that, you may be addicted to caffeine (don't laugh, many people are). Try reducing your intake and eliminating it entirely after mid-afternoon.

4. Exercise regularly. Exercise is good for just about everyone, particularly those suffering from stress. It helps in two main ways: You focus on the exercise and forget about the things that are causing the stress. And exercise prepares your body (mentally and physically) for coping better with stress. Exercise produces a 'training effect'. The act of exercising consumes a great deal more energy than sitting around, and your body adapts by storing more energy. The result is that you won't feel as tired during the day. And, at the end of the day, you'll also be able to sleep because you'll be physically as well as mentally tired.

You don't have to run a half-marathon every day or invest a fortune in lycra and gym membership fees. If you want to, fine, but there's really no need to become an exercise 'junkie'. Moderate exercise, like walking, four times a week for at least half an hour each time is enough.

Part of you will be thinking: 'But I hate exercise . . .'. This is a

feeble excuse: there's an unlimited variety of things that
constitute exercise. And it's not all like joining the SAS. There's
walking, jogging, aerobics, swimming, cycling, tennis, squash,
football, basketball, yoga, etc. Try it with an open mind; if you're
not careful, you may even find yourself having a good time.

5. Relax whenever you can. It's essential. It's simply not
possible to work flat out all the time, so set some time aside
every day just to relax. Be realistic – a couple of hours is more
than enough. Do something you really enjoy.

Some school or college students have a real problem with their
parents coming down on them like a ton of bricks if they're
caught relaxing. If you think you're one of these students, are
you really working hard enough? Be honest! If so, do your recent
exam results corroborate your answer? If you clearly are not
working hard enough, then the criticisms levelled at you are
valid. Meaning it's time to start working. If you are working
hard enough and your marks demonstrate this, you don't really
need to work harder. (But don't give yourself a week off for doing
such a great job, however.)

If you are really working hard and your marks are bad, you must
be doing something wrong. Don't work any harder, or spend
longer doing it – you must change the way you work so that it's
more effective. Have you been following all the study
suggestions earlier in this book? If not, it's time to start. If you
have, then you must clearly have a problem with the exams
themselves. And the cure for these is discussed in Chapter 3.

6. Avoid arguments, at school and at home. Arguing doesn't
help anyone. And it certainly doesn't put you in a very receptive
frame of mind for studying. It's easy to argue, particularly when
you're under stress, and often, it's very hard to walk away.
Walking away is the best option, however.

7. Talk to someone who might be receptive about your anxieties
– try someone who lives with you or your parents. If you're a
young adult (say, just finishing school or slightly older), your
parents are in a very difficult position, one which you can't fully

appreciate. You think you have problems, but think about theirs for a second: they've invested something like 20 years of their lives in you. During this time (often without one day off!) they have tried to provide you with everything you need to help you succeed. They can't, however, do the work or sit for the exams – that's up to you. And this makes parents feel left out and frustrated if you're not doing so well.

Help them (and, at the same time, yourself) by discussing your anxieties with them. They may not be able to say much that will be of direct assistance, but it might just get them off your back. And you might find it's a great help just to talk to someone about your problems. At the very least, talking about it will help you get your thoughts and feelings in the open.

8.   Learn some simple relaxation techniques. You don't have to go overboard with with Eastern-style philosophy or meditation – there's nothing mystical about it. The techniques that help are basically deep breathing exercises where you learn to release any stressful tensions that have built up during the day.

One of the biggest worries about stress is that you can't stop thinking about the things that worry you, even when you try to relax. Learning these relaxation techniques will help you to switch off, mentally, from the problems. You could even do a short course in relaxation or consult some of the many books on the subject.

People are all different, and we all react differently to stress. The trick is to know when stress is getting out of hand. You will find some of these suggestions more helpful than others. Use those that are most effective. Remember that everyone suffers from stress to varying degrees and you can do something constructive about it if your performance starts to suffer.

SUMMARY

Reduce stress by: eating well, being organised, reducing or eliminating caffeine, exercising regularly, learning to relax, avoiding arguments, and talking about problems.

☐ FAMILY AND FRIENDS

Exams place extra stress on your relationships with people close to you – family and friends. Most people are aware of this, but they never really do anything about it.

Like you, your family and friends like to relax whenever they can. And those routine, domestic tasks around home don't stop just because your exams are drawing inexorably closer. Vacuuming the floor, cooking the meal and mowing the lawn are still necessary. Unfortunately, you may feel that they unacceptably disrupt your study programme.

Family and friends are usually far more sympathetic to your needs than you may think. They've probably compensated for your exams by trying much harder than usual to avoid catching you off guard. Try to remember that they've got their own obligations and needs. And you have to make some concessions to their needs, too.

Most people, including you, are much less tolerant than usual as exams approach. Consider the number of arguments you find yourself a part of when you're not preparing for exams. Compare this to arguments around exam time. There are usually significantly more at exam time. What's different? You've got the same family and friends – the only difference is the stress you're under. The cause of these arguments is your exam stress. Think about that next time you're tempted to react in a hostile way.

If, on the other hand, you're reading this book to help a family member or friend who is a student:

Try to remember how difficult your important exams were. If you're normal, you would have found them awful at times. Likewise, you more than likely also acted in an anti-social or even hostile way to your family and friends. If you haven't experienced the dubious pleasure of sitting for major exams, try to imagine what it would be like to spend a year or more preparing for something you know you are going to find very demanding indeed.

SUMMARY

Coping with exams is a matter of give and take – both for you and for your family and friends.

DURING THE EXAMS

If you apply some of the suggestions in Chapter 2 to your study programme, you will be better prepared than ever before for the next exam. But there are a few extra things you should do to improve your performance on the day. And you can, and should, practise many of them weeks in advance of the exams.

Obviously, get enough sleep on the night before the exam and check the exam timetable repeatedly to confirm that the exams are indeed on when you think they are. You should also have all the required equipment packed well in advance and get up early so that you arrive on time. Intense revision on the night before exams doesn't help, it's better to revise the subject lightly and spend the remainder of the evening relaxing.

☐ THE BASICS

Do yourself a few favours before the exam starts:

1. Arrive at least 15 minutes early. Use this time to relax and think positively. It's extremely upsetting to place yourself under even more pressure by arriving late, and it won't help your marks. Plan for unexpected delays by allowing more travel time than you normally need. If you are late, you won't be given any extra exam time, even if you can come up with a really good excuse.

2. Don't spend too much time talking to your friends before the exam. These conversations are often quite negative – everyone usually tries to point out how little study they've done, how bad their mark will be, and how impossible the upcoming questions are sure to be. But while some people might find these last-minute conversations of some comfort, if you have applied yourself to your preparation you will want to do well and not be put off.

34

So if it helps – keep to yourself and think positively; think of yourself as one of the few students who is well prepared and knows what to expect. There will be plenty of time to chat after the exam.

When you take your seat and before the exam starts, write your name and all other required information on the paper that you expect to submit.

SUMMARY

1. **Arrive early.**
2. **No negative conversations.**

☐ WHEN YOU FINALLY START THE EXAM . . .

1. Always read the entire paper before you start answering the questions, even where reading time isn't formally given at the start. Why? Do it so each question won't be a big shock when you get to it. Make sure you have a complete question paper: have all of the pages been printed? It's no excuse to say: 'Questions 2 and 3 weren't on my paper'. Read the paper's directions to candidates several times; they are usually printed on the front cover.

Do you have to answer all of the questions or is there a choice? Are all of the questions worth equal marks? Are calculators allowed? Do you have to answer each question in a separate answer booklet? Is there a recognised area for rough working only? Will marks be deducted for careless or untidy working? Are you allowed access to written theory?

2. In some exams you must attempt all the questions; in others there may be a choice. Allocate a fixed amount of time for each question, based on the number of marks the question is worth. Go straight to the next question when that time is up, regardless

of whether or not you've finished (although this may be more difficult with essay-type exams – see below – where your time allocation must be equally strict). You can return to unfinished questions if you have time left over at the end.

A possible formula for those of you who like this kind of thing might be as follows:

$$\frac{\text{Time for this question} = \text{possible mark for this question}}{\text{total possible exam mark (usually 100)}} \times \text{total exam time}$$

Example

An exam paper may be divided (say) into into three sections, A, B, and C. Section A may be worth 20 marks, section B, 30 marks and section C, 50 marks (total = 100 marks). In order to divide your time between these sections fairly, 20% of the total time should be spent on section A, 30% on section B and 50% on section C.

SECTION	A	B	C
% TOTAL MARKS	20	30	50
TIME PER SECTION (in a three hour exam)	36 mins	54 mins	90 mins
START TIME	9.00am	9.36am	10.30am
FINISH TIME	9.36am	10.30am	12.00pm

In this example for a three-hour exam, allow 36 minutes for section A, 54 minutes for section B and 90 minutes for section C. If the exam starts at 8.50am with 10 minutes reading time, you start writing at 9.00am. If you elect to try section A first, scribble a quick note on the question paper that you must stop work on section A at 9.36am. If you do section B next, make a note to stop at 10.30am. After you've finished your preliminary run through sections A, B and C, you'll be in a position to attempt the questions you haven't answered yet (if you have any time left).

3. One word about finishing early. Most exams tend to keep you more than adequately occupied for the duration, so you'll rarely finish early. But if you do, don't leave the examination room

early (even if you've answered the whole paper) unless you're sure that your answers are correct. Use the unexpected spare time productively by revising your answers and correcting any mistakes you find along the way. Even five or six half-marks gained in this way can make a big difference.

If you finish early because you couldn't answer some of the questions, stay put! It's tempting to dash off, but instead, hang around and concentrate on the job at hand. Your only consideration should be to get more marks, so if you can remember any theory related to the questions you can't answer, write it down as the first line of your working. Then, at least, the examiner will know that you know something about the subject. Keep concentrating until the time runs out – you might surprise yourself by what you can achieve in this time.

4. Exams are often set out in such a way that it is usually comparatively easy to get the first few marks in each question but relatively hard to get the last few. So if you run out of time before attempting to answer all the questions, you miss out on the opportunity to earn the relatively easy marks at the beginning of some. Always write something down, even if you don't complete your answer: as a last resort, try a rough essay plan, a diagram or an equation that you know. This may well be worth a few marks in an exam, particularly if the questions are badly done by the majority of candidates. If you don't think it's worth the effort just for a few marks, tell that to someone who missed out on achieving their goal by just five marks!

5. If your answer is an essay (see below) and you run short of time, quickly complete the remainder in point form, so the examiner can see where you were heading, and what your conclusion(s) were. Remember that this, also, is a last resort only; you will always get more marks for the properly completed product.

6. Remember that it's often not essential that you answer each question in the order it appears in the question paper, although you can if this is the most convenient sequence. You can, and should, deviate from this sequence if there is a good reason to do

so. For example, it may be immediately obvious how to solve questions 1, 6 and 8. If so, do them first, and address the others later. Doing the exam this way will really help your confidence as you work through the exam. The other advantage is, of course, that you won't be leaving any easy questions until near the end, when you may be short of time. Remember, everyone is different and the best sequence for you may not be the same as the order in which the questions are printed.

7. It's very easy to lose marks by forgetting to answer a question. How would you feel if you missed out on your goal by one or two marks and then discovered that ten marks or more were lost because you left out a question by mistake? You must develop an idiot-proof method which ensures this does not happen! Therefore, as you finish each question, place an obvious cross over it on the question paper. You will then have a quick, accurate visual reference regarding which questions remain to be answered.

8. Two final short pieces of advice: Ask the supervisor about anything you're unsure of, no matter how trivial. And double-check to ensure that all of your answers are submitted with your name (and number, if appropriate) on them.

SUMMARY

1. **Read the paper first.**
2. **Know the rules.**
3. **Attempt all the questions (ie all which must be answered).**
4. **Allocate the time sensibly.**
5. **Never leave early.**
6. **Never leave a question out by mistake.**

☐ EXAM QUESTIONS

Many students believe that examiners, as a group, get their

kicks by taking away as many of your marks as they can possibly justify. This is not the case. Most examiners try very hard to give students as many marks as they can. And you can help make their job a whole lot easier by presenting your answer neatly.

As previously discussed, well-presented answers get more marks. Unfair, maybe, but true. If you want better marks, you must devote some time during your exam preparation to improving the presentation of your answers. You cannot possibly prepare untidy, poorly presented answers while studying and then turn out perfectly presented answers during exams. It just doesn't happen. Well-presented answers are the result of disciplined, ordered thoughts and of practice – and you must develop the habit of good presentation before doing important exams.

Place yourself in the examiner's position: they have the rather difficult job of trying to interpret hundreds of answers to the same questions. If you get the final answer wrong, the examiner then tries to award some marks for the correct portion of your working. The examiner will try a lot harder if your answers are neat and easy to understand. If this task proves impossible, the examiner will have no option other than giving you zero for that question.

Good presentation includes neat writing, clear diagrams, uncluttered spacing and a logical flow or progression through each answer. Where possible, begin each question on a new page and clearly indicate the question number on the top of the page. Diagrams should be at least half a page in size and all relevant components should be clearly labelled. Paper is very cheap by comparison to poor exam marks which are very costly – so spread out your working and make it look neat. Do this even if you are against the wanton destruction of the world's forests to provide paper. If you get the right marks, you may well be able to place yourself in a good position actually to do something about it.

SUMMARY

Help the examiner to help you – presentation counts!

☐ ESSAY ANSWERS

There's a certain vagueness about the way most people are taught to write essays. Students either pick it up straight away or they don't. If you are one of those that haven't quite made the connection, there's a 'cookbook' way of approaching essay writing. It may not be the ideal way to write essays, but it will get you out of the starting blocks, and further practice will refine your technique until it's satisfactory.

Your essay must be organised before you bolt down the page in a mad rush to get as many words scribbled down as possible. Many essays will undoubtedly be a feature of any sensible study plan, and it would definitely be a good idea to practise the cookbook procedure then. If you already earn high marks for your essays, don't change anything!

Here's the recipe:

1. Read the question at least twice, more if necessary. Underline or highlight the key words. Make sure you understand the question! The appendix on page 54 gives a number of key words which are commonly used in exam questions, together with their precise meaning.

2. Most essays ask for your opinion. They say 'Discuss . . .', '. . . do you agree?', 'Does . . .', or whatever (see appendix). Decide what your opinion is. Be definite – you can't change horses half-way through!

3. Quickly list, on scrap paper, the points you think support your opinion. Re-read your list and cross out any of these that

don't really get your point of view across. Delete also those points you can't justify with examples or quotes.

4. On your answer sheet write the words 'Essay Plan'. Then list (in order) the points that you're going to address. This is the start of your essay; it helps you get your thoughts organised and, just as importantly, it's a road map for the examiner which does more than merely indicate that you started your brain before you got your pen into gear.

5. Start writing your essay. Your introduction should be a clear, concise, logical one-paragraph statement outlining your position. You are saying words to the effect of: 'This is my opinion and I will be using specific examples from the text(s) to justify it'. The only difference is that you write it formally, in the third person. That is, do not use the word 'I', as in 'I will show . . .'. Use instead, for example: 'It is clear that . . . (whatever)', or, 'Many references in the text support the view that . . . (whatever)'. However, do not include specific information (references, quotes or examples) in your introduction. These come next.

6. Refer to your essay plan and discuss your points systematically. Begin each point with a new paragraph. Remember, the reason for writing about these points is to justify your opinion to the examiner. So your job is to put the specific point you raise into context, explaining exactly why it supports your viewpoint. Keep this firmly in mind throughout the essay.

When you re-read your essay, you may see that some things you've written don't quite provide the justification you want; either change them so they do or get rid of them altogether. Anything that doesn't support your opinion is waffle and it will affect your final mark. Examiners hate waffle – therefore be concise and use specific information to justify your argument. Conversely, examiners love relevant quotes, diagrams, figures or examples used in essays.

7. Conclude your essay. Your conclusion should be a logical, one-paragraph statement which outlines the fact that your

viewpoint has been justified. You should not, however, merely
re-jig your introduction. The difference is that the introduction
says the formal equivalent of: '. . . my opinion is . . . and I'm
going to justify it using examples' whereas the conclusion says
the formal equivalent of: 'The examples used show that my
opinion is justified'.

8. Read back your essay and ask yourself if you have justified
your opinion adequately. Make any necessary changes.
Remember that most exam essays are written in a single draft.
That is, you don't generally have time to write them, perform
major surgery on them to get them right and then re-write a
corrected version. Getting essays pretty much right on the first
go is a skill that can only be developed with practice.

A word about being too definite. You usually do not have to prove
that the viewpoint you've taken is the only correct one. That is,
you don't have to say, or demonstrate, than any other view is
wrong. Despite the fact that you may believe yours is the only
correct opinion, that's not what you're being asked to prove.
What you are being asked to do is merely justify an opinion
using specific facts. Therefore, never say the formal equivalent
of: 'I've shown that my opinion is absolutely correct' (this implies
that any other opinion is wrong). In most essays, you could select
either point of view and receive the same marks as long as your
justifications are sound. (It's rather like a political debate or a
court case where either side can use the same facts to justify
opposite points of view!)

As a general guide to writing style, always write in the third
person (don't say 'I'). Use simple words and phrases to get the
point across. The words you use should be almost like speech.
When you first start, the bigger cumbersome words tend to build
convoluted phrases . . . and then you risk becoming muddled and
confusing to the examiner. Remember to use sentences,
paragraphs and correct grammar. (If you don't know how to use
commas and apostrophes, or how to punctuate quotes, you
should try and find out beforehand by consulting some books on
correct punctuation or by asking your teacher/lecturer – these
skills are essential.) Examiners tend to be impressed when

students use a variety of connecting words instead of 'and'. You should try incorporating the following connecting words/phrases into your vocabulary: thus, in addition, as, further, therefore, hence, however, etc. Sadly, you can't merely go through your essay and cross out two out of every three 'ands', and replace them with the options listed. These options all have grammatical conventions associated with them which you must observe. In other words, incorporate them, where appropriate, into your essay as you write. Above all, stick to the point!

Spell the names of all characters and places correctly. (Proper nouns such as these all begin with capital letters – so do sentences!) And don't let your handwriting degenerate into an illegible scrawl – if you feel a need to scrawl illegibly, pause momentarily and stretch your writing hand and arm.

If you really have trouble writing essays, ask a teacher for help or buy a book on essay writing. (There are plenty on the market – or try your local library.) But the major component to essay improvement is the same as in any other activity – practise, as often as possible. Get an interested teacher or other competent person to review critically your practice essays.

SUMMARY

1. **Justify your opinion.**
2. **Re-read and make necessary corrections.**
3. **Don't be over-definite.**
4. **Be clear and concise.**
5. **Learn to use correct style and grammar.**
6. **Stick to the point!**

☐ TECHNICAL ANSWERS

These are answers that require mathematical calculations or other similar types of logical presentation. Answers in physics, chemistry and other sciences fall into this category.

Answering questions in these subjects is just like learning to speak another language. There is a loosely conventional way of answering these questions:

1. Read the question twice. Look for the given information and the thing you have to find. It's important to realise that you don't have to know what the answer is, but you have to be pretty sure of the best way to start your solution and how to progress towards the answer. If you don't understand the question, read on.

2. Write down the given data, under the heading 'Given:'. Write down the thing you have to find, under the heading 'Find:'. If relevant, draw a diagram, even if you can't immediately see the point. Write down relevant formulae that you know. This is not a waste of time because it demonstrates that you understand the question and know the relevant theory (you get marks for knowing this). It also helps you to get your thoughts organised before you plunge into the working.

3. Write down the heading 'Solution:'. Have a careful look at what you've got to work with. The clues are all there, believe it or not: in a way, it's telling you to do something. The trick is to figure out the most logical thing to do. (People who are effectively prepared will find this easier than people who aren't.) Each line of your solution hides a clue that tells you how to get to the next line. Keep going, finding more clues and writing more lines, and observing the conventions learned in class and reinforced during study – when you can't go any further, you're at the answer.

Examiners love to see logical things written down. If you know your answer is wrong, don't ignore this fact. Write something nearby like, 'I suspect a mistake – check later if time allows'. This tells the examiner that you know enough about the subject to suspect things aren't going according to plan. You are allowed to use words amid technical answers, so explain clearly what you're doing. Words like 'integrating', 'subbing into', 'differentiating', 'Pythagoras', 'solving simultaneously' etc., when applied appropriately, make your answer seem less like a meaningless page of hieroglyphics. Keep all of your '=' signs in a straight line down the page. Leave a blank line in between each line of working. Clearly indicate your answer by underlining it at the end.

SUMMARY

1. **Sort out the given data and the thing you have to do from the question.**
2. **Include both theory and words in your answer.**
3. **Apply logic and experience to find the most efficient solution.**

☐ DIFFICULT QUESTIONS

Unfortunately, no matter how well prepared you are, or how hard you've studied, some questions will present an unforeseen problem: how to do them won't be immediately obvious. This happens in essay-type exams and in technical exams. And it happens regardless of your level of ability. You need a quick method of dealing with these problems.

Most candidates for technical subjects have a novel way of dealing with questions that they can't interpret. They play around a bit in the vain hope that the answer will simply fall out. In the overwhelming majority of cases, it doesn't. If you choose the 'play around' method, the odds certainly aren't in your favour: there is only one correct answer and an infinity of wrong ones.

Candidates who can't interpret essay questions usually answer a question which they think is nearly the same as the one that's been asked. They kid themselves that the examiner won't notice the difference. This, too, is a flawed strategy because the examiner gets far more practice noticing the difference than you do at disguising it.

45

Exam questions always contain two main pieces of information. These are the given data and the thing the examiner wants you to do. You may think that only technical subjects are like this. In reality, however, questions in all exams must conform to this format. Essays questions, for example, always ask you to do something and they always give you something specific to work with. It's good that all questions are similarly structured – it means that you can approach them all in basically the same way.

The given data

Every exam question contains all of the data required to solve the problem. There is never too little, although sometimes extra, unnecessary information is included which may be a little confusing. Your job is to find all of the required data, some of which the examiner may have subtly hidden, lest every candidate gets 100 per cent. If you keep reading, you will eventually get to the important point of the question.

The thing the examiner wants you to do

This is the actual thing which you have to do in order to get the marks. It sounds really obvious when you think about it but the examiner sometimes also makes this hard to interpret, also for the above reason.

Here's how to get from a confusing question to a clear, concise list of the relevant data in a science question (but remember to complete all the easy questions first!):

1. Read the question twice. Do it slowly, phrase by phrase. Try to get inside the examiner's head – what does he/she want? What is she/he giving you to start the ball rolling? But don't worry if it's all still a mystery.

2. Start your answer by writing down all the given data in a neat list. Go through the question systematically and you'll find most of the given data will become obvious. More than likely, the examiner will require you to interpret some of the question and make a logical conclusion, in the process turning an otherwise

useless phrase into a concrete piece of datum. An example of this would be where a question says: 'A point lies on the y-axis'. The conclusion you must draw to extract the useful datum is that the x-value of the point is zero.

If you prefer, you can cross out (lightly, in pencil) each piece of given data and associated joining words as you write them down. Draw a neat diagram, including any relevant data, even if you doubt it will be helpful. Do this because the diagram will help you to interpret the given data. Also, you may get some marks for the diagram, even if you can't solve the problem.

3. Write down exactly what the examiner wants you to do. This is what you'll be left with if you've crossed out all the given data and joining words.

4. Review what you've done in steps 2 and 3. The information you have in front of you should fit neatly into some formula, essay plan or other theory that you've studied. The rest of the answer should fall into place from here. If it doesn't, don't give up – review what you've done and if nothing springs to mind, find another hard question and give it a go.

Never say 'this question can't be done' and then move quickly on to the next question without doing any working. Questions are either easy or difficult, but never impossible. Clearly, every question can be done! You must try seriously to get at least some marks for each question and you can't get any marks without writing something on the paper!

If a question is particularly difficult, many of the other candidates will leave it out completely, submitting no working at all. In this case, the markers will probably award marks for merely getting the given data, diagrams and theory correct.

SUMMARY

1. **Difficult questions are a fact of life.**
2. **You must train yourself to deal with them quickly and efficiently.**
3. **Never just play around, or answer a slightly different question.**
4. **Separate the given information and the thing that's required, then proceed logically, using the theory you know.**

☐ MENTAL AND PHYSICAL FATIGUE

Get used to the fact that you'll be feeling pretty exhausted towards the end of the exam. But console yourself with the fact that you'll feel better than most other students if you've studied in a way that simulates the exam. Nothing, however, prepares you 100 per cent for exams – except, maybe, having passed many beforehand. The fatigue you feel can be either mental or physical, or a combination of both.

You've experienced physical fatigue – it's when your writing hand starts to ache and cramp up (usually with at least one more essay still to do). You might also get some back or neck pain caused by hunching over the paper for a couple of hours.

Physical fatigue is easy to cure. Simply stop writing regularly for a few seconds at a time. If your hand hurts, extend it and stretch it into a comfortable position for a moment. Look up at the ceiling and stretch up straight to ease your back. Take a few deep breaths and relax. You'll feel much better after a few seconds. Do it regularly during the exam and you'll have much more stamina, particularly towards the end of the paper.

Mental fatigue is when you can't get the ideas to flow properly and you feel like you've just been forcefully woken up in the middle of the night. Pausing briefly (and regularly) to relieve physical fatigue also helps relieve mental fatigue. But the main factor that affects mental fatigue is relaxation and thorough preparation. Mental fatigue is caused when you have extended yourself far beyond the normal limits of your attention span. So if you completed numerous study sessions where you effectively simulated exam conditions, and especially if you completed many past papers, each without interruption, you will find yourself in a much better mental position towards the end of the exam. You'll finish the exam wondering how three hours could have possibly passed so quickly.

SUMMARY

1. **Some fatigue is inevitable, but it can be minimised.**
2. **Cure physical fatigue by relaxing and stretching regularly.**
3. **Cure mental fatigue by being effectively prepared.**

☐ MORE THAN ONE EXAM?

Most students aren't merely forced to cope with an exam, they're forced to contend with several. And these can be spread over an intense few days, or over several weeks.

Once you've finished an exam, it's over. You can't alter what's past, so concentrate on the upcoming exams. Don't re-live what went wrong, or wonder whether this answer or that was right. It won't achieve anything. Direct your energies to where they will make a difference – the exams you haven't yet done.

Also, don't waste too much time talking about the exam afterwards. Exam post mortems are usually pointless – they're negative and absolutely counter-productive. After the exam, go home and relax. If your timetable allows, take the rest of the day off. Whether you can, in practice, do this obviously depends on the time remaining until the next exam. But most people can't study effectively immediately after an exam.

Starting on the day after the exam, it's your job to become motivated for the next one. Don't mess around – get straight to work. Make sure your preparation is adequate for each exam – are they all worth a similar amount towards your final assessment? Don't fall into the trap of letting your preparation slide at the last minute.

There's no real secret recipe for instilling yourself with self-motivation after a week of exams with at least another week still to go. Just keep doing what you (hopefully) did during the earlier part of the preparation phase. That is, work sensibly and hard for an intelligent amount of time and then relax. And keep thinking about your goal – that's the reason you're putting yourself through this, right?

Some unfortunate students sit for a fairly intensive block of exams at the beginning of the exam period and are then left with a week or more to endure until their last exam. Most of their friends are already out making up for lost social life and this select few still have the sword of Damocles hanging over their head. If you find yourself in this position, put things in perspective. You may recently have had eight or more major exams to contend with, and now there's only one. Two to three hours a day of intensive preparation is enough. Start early, say 8.30am, and you'll be finished before lunch. You will then have the rest of the day to go out and most of your friends will still be feeling rotten from the night before!

Unfortunately though, late nights and getting generally run down from too much of a good time are still off-limits until you finish completely. Then you can really enjoy the luxury of total relaxation. Amaze your friends then with your ability to party – they'll all be needing a quiet rest by this stage.

SUMMARY

1. **Exams usually attack in groups.**
2. **Try to relax after each one.**
3. **Don't re-live the last exam, concentrate on the upcoming ones.**
4. **Try to keep the pressure on right until the very end.**

☐ FINALLY ...

The advice you have been given should help you prepare for our exams well in advance. All you must do now is prove to yourself that you have the discipline to apply what you've read about and get the marks you need.

But it is true that you can only improve by *applying* the principles you've recently learned. Organise yourself and get your study act together today. Try keeping this book close by so that you can refer to it as the need arises. You may find it helpful to re-read some sections as the exams approach.

The other fact of life, as explained at the very beginning, is that you'll probably always hate exams. But consider the alternative: is it possible to like them? They are just a necessary part of the game for those who want to achieve more in life.

Remember that the sole purpose for existence isn't to study. Study is necessary, but other aspects of your life are equally important. A balanced combination of study, work, rest and fun works best for most of us. A healthy diet, some regular exercise, plenty of sleep, a good social life and a genuine attempt to be nice to your family all help. This sounds like an endorsement for a brand-name breakfast cereal, but really, if you maintain a balanced lifestyle, it reduces the impact of the times when you inevitably 'forget' to study, go AWOL or generally behave a little irresponsibly at times.

Books and teachers help you learn, but the responsibility for your performance rests solely with you. This is an immense responsibility which you must shoulder with the utmost care. Exam marks can determine the direction that the rest of your life will take. You owe it to yourself to get your study act together and it really is up to you. *Start doing it TODAY!*

☐ CHECKLISTS

1. Eight weeks before major exams

- My diet is OK. I'm getting regular exercise and adequate sleep. I feel like the stress is under control.
- My revision timetable is updated (and written below).
- The duration of my revision is at least two hours per night.
- I'm conducting revision at least five times per week (in each subject).
- My study notes are complete and organised.
- I have access to many exam-style revision questions.
- I've re-read this book and decided how I can maximise my performance.

2. Four weeks before major exams

- I'm still doing the things I started in checklist 1.
- I have identified my weaknesses and I'm concentrating on overcoming these.
- I'm certain of the topics that will be addressed in the exams.
- I have arranged my revision programme so that it suits the exam topics.

3. One week before major exams

- I'm absolutely certain of the exam timetable.

- I'm absolutely certain of the format of each exam.
- I'm absolutely certain of the requirements for each exam.
- I'm not allowing myself to get physically run down or overtired.
- I'm eating healthy food and I am getting enough sleep.

4. The night before major exams

- I'm absolutely sure the exam I *think* is on tomorrow is the exam which is *actually* on tomorrow.
- My bag is packed with all of the required equipment.
- I'm going to get enough sleep tonight.
- I've planned my trip tomorrow so that I'll arrive at least 15 minutes early.
- I've allowed some time for any delays which may occur.
- I'm going to spend the rest of the night relaxing and I'm not doing any more study tonight.

5. Exam day checklist

- I have re-checked the details of today's exams.
- I have re-checked that I've packed everything I'll need.
- I ate a light, healthy breakfast.
- I left home in plenty of time for an early arrival.

APPENDIX

Words commonly used in set questions

Make sure you understand what is required by reading the question carefully. Terms used vary in their precise meaning and you should pay particular attention to what is required:

Account for – explain.

Analyse – describe the elements of a particular issue, idea, etc and criticise.

Argue the case for – use reasoned argument to support a particular point of view.

Assess – weigh up the pros and cons of a particular point of view to determine its strength or value.

Calculate – mathematical computation or reckoning.

Comment upon – offer your opinion on . . . (avoiding the use of 'I').

Compare – highlight the similarities between things; sometimes this implies drawing attention to the differences too.

Consider – draw together some observations and opinions about something.

Contrast – put two or more concepts, ideas or issues in opposition so that differences can be highlighted.

Criticise – make an assessment of the relative truth or weight of particular facts or theories, your judgement supported by discussion of the evidence.

Define – give the precise meaning of something, showing how you have done so.

Describe – give an account of something with some detail.

Discuss – give an explanation of a topic but from different points of view, for and against, with your reasons.

APPENDIX

Distinguish between – point out the differences among examples.

Evaluate – give your appraisal on the worth of something with supporting facts and arguments.

Examine – make an investigation or an enquiry into something.

Explain – account for something, revealing and explaining its elements or arguments.

Explore – look at an issue in a questioning manner.

Give an account of – provide a detailed description of something.

Illustrate – clarify by the use of concrete examples (or use a diagram).

Interpret – make explicit the meaning of . . . with supporting argument.

Justify – show reasoning for conclusions and/or arguments.

Outline – summarise the main features of a subject – emphasising its structure rather than its detailed elements.

Relate – highlight how things are connected to each other, or occasionally, to narrate something.

Review – make a critical examination or survey of a subject.

State – give a clear and brief presentation of something.

Summarise – give a precise account of something, highlighting key points rather than detailed examples.

Trace – from a point of origin, show the history or development of an issue.

What . . . When . . . Where . . . Why – these are often used. Make sure you answer appropriately.

Some questions combine two of these key terms such as: 'Compare and contrast' or 'Describe and explain . . .'. In some essay-type subjects such as in the humanities and social sciences you should watch out for whether the causes or reasons

for something (e.g. 'Account for . . .' or 'What problems faced . . .')
or the results of something ('What was the impact of . . .', 'How
successful/important was . . .') are required in your answers.

FURTHER READING

Exam skills & school exams information

How to Pass Exams Without Anxiety, David Acres, Northcote House, 3rd edition 1994.

How to Succeed In A Levels, Howard Barlow, Kogan Page, 2nd edition 1991.

Your GCSE Decisions, Alan Vincent, Trotman, 1993.

Study skills

Effective Studying, Steve Robertson and David Smith, Longman 1987.

How to Study, Harry Maddox, Penguin, revised 1988.

How to Study, A. D. Burgen, Harrap, 1982.

How to Study: A Practical Guide, Francis Casey, Macmillan, 1985.

How to Study Effectively, Carol Harman and Richard Freeman, National Extension College, 1984.

How to Win As a Part-Time Student: A Study Skills Guide, Tom Bourner and Phil Race, Kogan Page, 1990.

Mastering Study Skills, R. Freeman, Macmillan, 1982.

Study! A Guide to Effective Study, Revision and Examinations, Robert Barrass, Chapman & Hall, 1984.

Study and Learn, S. Ashman and A. George, Heinemann, 1982.

Student guides

Mature Students' Guide, Trotman, 1994.

The Student Book 1995, Klaus Boehm and Jenny Lees-Spalding, Macmillan, 1994.

The Time Out/NUS Student Guide, Time Out, 1991.

Memorising techniques & stress management

Make the Most of Your Memory, Gwen Ansell, National Extension College, 1984.

Taking the Strain, R. Eagle, BBC Publications, 1982.